On Every Stone

On Every Stone

RACHEL VIGIER

Pedlar Press | TORONTO

PEDLAR PRESS
PO Box 26, Station P, Toronto Ontario M5S 2S6 Canada

ACKNOWLEDGEMENTS. The publisher gratefully acknowledges the financial support of the Canada Council for the Arts and the Ontario Arts Council for its publishing program.

Edited for the press by Molly Peacock.

NATIONAL LIBRARY OF CANADA CATALOGUING IN PUBLICATION

Vigier, Rachel
        On every stone / Rachel Vigier.

Poems.
ISBN 0-9686522-9-8

        I. Title.

PS8593.I3S06 2002   c811'.6   C2002-903323-3
PR9199.4.V5306 2002

First Edition

COVER ART Wayne McNulty
COVER & BOOK DESIGN Zab Design & Typography

Printed in Canada

For my sister

For my family

What we remember
is lost by half every time —

On Every Stone

CONTENTS

DISAPPEARED

I am disappeared and you come looking for me as I knew you would.
I may be dead or not. Do you know by now it is all the same?

Up here you think I am alone but I am not. Some nights there are stars.
I head for high ground. Somewhere you will read this is what lost people do.

I know you will search my work—crazy stories—some written backwards,
All for the sake of safety. I know you will find every word that matters

Markers for a grave I never left behind.

ON EVERY STONE

OCTOBER

It starts with a faraway sun
and burnished leaves
skittering across

a gravel road. I ask you
to take my hand
and stay. Tell me

how long will it take
to come back
from the sharp inhale

of rotted leaves,
the stubbled fields,
the garden of empty stalks?

GIVEN

I see you running or falling to the sin
of destruction, your back bent to break

with the branches driving you low
or the current driving you under

I want to hold you to this earth
and say this is a place we can know.

Why did you give up — or were you tricked?
— a heartless flash, suddenly one step

too far and you're gone, given to the river
or the woods even beyond the smell of dogs.

DISAPPEAR

To pass out of sight, vanish;
to cease to be, or exist;
also, to get lost,

especially without warning
or explanation. Disappear
as applied to objects,

a cloud disappeared; or
to people, to cause (someone)
to disappear. *Ex.* in Chile

thousands disappeared,
were disappeared; or reflexively
one sister disappeared herself. And,

one can now speak of the state
of being disappeared, how
the disappeared disappear.

SOME DAYS

I face the direction
that lost you
and ask for a body
some bones
a set of teeth
to match
number to name
formally
close the case
the missing tag
neatly folded
marking the edge
you walked off

TO THE RIVER

The day you disappeared I went to the United Nations.
I entered the great assembly, a half-circle of some power
where Golda once spoke her mind, where Arafat stood
that first time still strapped to his gun. That day
the room was not yet ready to receive Nelson.
You would have liked this room with its carousel of leaders,
Plus ça change ma chère, we would have laughed.

Outside in the plaza, I think we might have argued
about the statue — that larger-than-life gun
with a larger-than-life barrel knotted up.
At first, you would have accepted it as a sign of peace.
I would have argued, the trigger is still there,
and eventually you would have agreed, coming up
with a sign or two of your own. Then hand in hand
we might have strolled through the garden to the river.

SWEET AND SOUR

I begin to eat my soup, sweet and sour,
at a Chinese restaurant where you talk
about the pictures on the wall, women
with tiny feet sitting alone in grand sedans.
Are they strangers, you ask the waiter,
or pictures of your grandmother taken
out of China? The soup comes as you reach
into your pocket. You show me two pills.

It's what they put in batteries, you say
as casually as you can. Your hand shakes,
lithium, the word makes you laugh. And then
you get angry in the old way. *It will turn
my piss to blood!* you shout to everyone.
I continue to eat, the soup sweet and sour.

BURNT GROUND

On this street, a powdery dust
settles on my shoulders
as I think of the moment — just before

when it's still an ordinary morning
on a bright September day
when the skyline

stretches up forever
the glory of space
standing still as workers

milling inside or on the street
each start an ordinary day
in an ordinary way. Now

this is the moment — just after
when I think whose dust is this
blowing across burnt ground?

ORDINARY
INTERRUPTIONS

My youngest daughter is asleep. I can finally look at her. She has been tossing and turning beside me, tired but fighting sleep. So I've kept my eyes closed, trying to set an example. Every once in a while I look to see if her eyes are still open. All the while I've been thinking about your disappearance, a kind of death without really being a death.

Of course, I've been reading your notebooks again. This time I'm not afraid. I can see the same kind of words I might write, just to get something down on the page.

In towards the end everything hardened even as free zones everywhere were being discussed. People decided to enjoy what they had and not have it all blow away in a puff of the huff. As I was visiting the whaling wall myself I heard it all too clearly. Unless something happened to stop it bodies would be washing up my shores. I check the butcher shops every morning for pink meat.

Is this your mind? Were you crazy? Am I crazy?

My oldest daughter, back from shopping with her father, stands beside me swinging her pillow and sucking her thumb. I wish you could know these ordinary interruptions.

I tell her I'm writing a message to my sister. "Can I help you?" she asks. She holds the pen as I write saying, "There you go. There you go," in a comforting, encouraging voice.

Sometimes I hope I am being watched
Sometimes I hope you are not alone
Sometimes I hope you went quickly

I know that's not true. I remember the years of pain and the story that finally undid me. You call at 3 a.m. to tell me about the state trooper who sodomized you and infected you with AIDS. There is no evidence of an attack. *Except for your words.* I don't know what to believe. *Except for your words.*

My daughter takes the pen away from me. "Are you finished?" she asks. Her sister continues to sleep.

ON EVERY STONE

In the first dream   I bury my face
in the earth   the natural sound
of rock calling rock
in heavy layers
and underground rivers   Now I remember
you always called   below the surface
a shivering echo   trace elements
working the roots

In the next dream   I open my mouth
to seed and soil   the language of the land
we walked   sisters every acre
working the earth that needed
moving stones across a field

                Now out of dreams
lost stones between us   make lonely sounds
In this field nothing moves   Back on the surface
I'm packing dreams   against hard earth
writing   *sister*   on every stone

STRANGE BONES

The dog chews a big knobby thighbone.
Some bones dried dirty in the sun.
Others bleached a smooth silvery grey.
These strange bones disturb us.

The formal voice at the end of the line
pauses, "The bones are 100 miles
from where she disappeared. Certainly
female." I want to ask the formal voice —

Did the skull vibrate? Did the ribs
lift and shake? Did the pelvis,
did the pelvis rock and rock
with pleasure when you touched it?

No? Then these strange bones
are not my sister.

NAMES

Suddenly it's important to know names —
the name of the waitress in the donut shop
the name of the clerk in the bookstore
the name of the teller at the bank
the name of the visitor in the elevator
the name of the guard at the door
the name of the janitor on the top floor
and in the park across the street
the names of all the old men
shuffling backgammon pieces
the names of all the office workers
jostling in lines by the food carts
even the name of the park and the name
of the statue in the park now covered in ash

MISSING

Year after year
the image
ages on its own
to show how crooked
a smile can become
how deep a dimple
can form in the skin.

If I were your mother
I'd see what was left
find the image
or die
sleeping in a room
where dreams
almost never come back.

KADDISH ON THE SPOT

It used to be
the body went
to the graveyard.

Now the body
stays where it's piloted
and the prayers

waft overhead
with the ashes
of one and all.

TENDER ARTIFACTS

THE GIFT

1

A glittering sky, a gazelle bounding
through a long-grass plain, a mind

lost slowly, ending suddenly
in the silence of a territory, *somewhere*

where it is no longer we who speak
but where, in our absence, we are spoken.

2

The hospital gown did not fit. The nurses
could not say your name so you gave yourself

a new and simple name. Rose, you said.
It is a new and simple name. On the horizon

the gazelle lingers as they make simple
sounds, try some talk in simple phrases. "Mas-

3

culine-looking, sullen and angry for no ap-
parent reason." On the lined page

of reason's report their voices wither. They cannot
speak you *ma fille de campagne* my *folle compagne.*

On the horizon the gazelle looks back, leaps
out of history, takes her young with her.

37

TIGHTROPE

I see you crossing Niagara Falls
on a tightrope —
arms extended, with no warning
the balancing pole tossed end-to-end.

No Great Blondin, you are not
blindfolded, making an omelette,
pushing a wheelbarrow or
carrying a passenger. Your crossing

is not a stunt. Eyes set
you thrive —
one slippery foot after another
on a line above churning water.

TENDER ARTIFACTS

1

My sister wrote on whatever
happened to be at hand. This folder

holds a menu from The Sleeping Lady
in Marin County, flyers

from a local laundromat and a painting
streaked rust and blue, all with words

scrawled on the back. *Shaking
shadows from a wall, following*

*shimmering reflections in the marble face
of a building that remains*

*while spitting pebbles on the riverbank.
Who will take*

these words, on faith? And on the edge
in tiny script — *J'ai souvent mal*

à la tête. Tu dois me croire. Je suis. Folle.

2

Every time I read her words
I'm thrown back
to what I don't know,

the mind
loosening itself
in a crevice of thought,

or a faultline
in the syntax of behaviour,
as I follow her hand, first

swooping over pages
then cramped
tight on an edge

going back
to a mother
tongue.

THE ABC OF GENIUS

Our mother is sifting through the remains again.
"Do you understand what your sister wrote?" she asks,

weighing my sister's notebook
on a balance

swinging somewhere in the skull, banging
against the bone or hanging

in a matrix of cells. Who's to tell?
Is this the ABC of genius,

the moment before the equation
when the old system crumbles in the cortex

or just cells
cracking across a fold of the brain

forcing crazy patterns
on the pages we hold between us?

AN ILLNESS
LIKE ANY OTHER

It's an illness like any other, Van Gogh wrote,
as the flashes behind his eyes kept popping,
while in his hands the brush's determination
to continue exploded beyond the canvas, hands
and eyes, together, wrestling the mind
into some kind of submission. The glory of it
assaulted him every time. *I have been working*
on a size 20 canvas in the open air in an orchard,
lilac plowland, a reed fence, two pink peach trees
against a sky of glorious blue and white.
On a size 20 canvas where illness equals work,
there is nothing more or less than hands,
brushes and eyes, scraping pink, lavender,
blue and white zinc here and there
until the mind in her illness settles
at the edge of an orchard
shedding blossoms in brilliant light.

SUDDEN RAIN: THE SUICIDE OF VIRGINIA WOOLF

Did you watch the river run over your shoes
rocks rattling round your ankles

before stooping to pick up the stone
with both hands, it was that heavy?

Then did you hold it for a long time,
not feeling its true weight

but gauging the shape, narrow at one end
so it must fit

perfectly in the pocket of your coat
as you shifted to hold the sudden weight with your hip

before taking one step and then another
into the river, your coat swelling around you

like a desert plant gorged by a sudden rain?

IN OUR OLD ROOM

In our old room
huddled between cold sheets
the frost comes at us.
Your face seems innocent
even with all the lies
you intend to tell.
You try to explain
some noise in your head
the sum of Paris, Vietnam
and America, the fist
barrelling into your head.
You try to explain
he was an old soldier
you picked up
an old wound from America
lost in Paris after the war.
You try to explain
how one night
you stood in
for the enemy
until the gun
swung to your head
and you had to run
for the only life you had
home with a typewriter
an old umbrella
and a debt to greedy cousins
your own wounds
by now purple shadows
lighting flares behind your eyes.

THE SIMPLICITY OF PLAY

I want to write about my sister and craziness and how a line
can define the point of disappearance

but I think about the girls instead. How this morning
they called across to each other from over their father

stretched out in a final cry of sleep
rolling over to catch them both in a fierce embrace

the first of the morning
the whole family tumbling into each other.

Tonight the girls teach each other the alphabet
spelling their names backwards on a frosted windowpane

as snow blankets the city. I remember the simplicity of play
with my sister, running circles

in fresh snow, the wind
slapping our cheeks, making tracks across an endless land

we meant to leave and leave again.
From the street we hear the sound of a shovel scraping the sidewalk

scraping a path straight through the snow.

DEAR LAND

SNOW ANGELS

The first snow always excites us —
No matter what time it is, our mother
always lets us out. I am the youngest.
You are the oldest. I hold up my foot.
You buckle my boot. This time it is night.
The moon floats in a clear sea of light.
The cold takes us down. We open our arms
and fight back laughing. I look up
and lose myself — somewhere there is a star
travelling. *Remember*, you call, *the trick
is to get up without losing the angel*.

THE FIRE

That spring my sister set the woods on fire.
The trees burned as the men talked
by the water tank waiting to be filled.
She would not speak and our father
would not look at her. That morning
she had shown me through the woods
to the pond full of shivering frog eggs,
the black clot at the centre of every cell.
I take her hand. We walk past our father
as close to the fire as our mother allows.
We look back to see the men spray
the smouldering grass, the charred trees
criss-crossed at the edge of the woods,
somewhere in there the scorched pond.

        Twenty years later
I stand with my mother and father
as we look north and see that the woods
are all gone, the land scraped raw
by a bulldozer and the neighbour's need
for a few more acres. We think
how you are gone too, disappeared
by a raw need of your own. My father calls,
The pond is gone. My mother asks,
Why did you do this thing? And I, *in memory*,
hold your hand, both of us shivering
against an old fire, a sizzling pond
and clots of jelly smeared to our shirts.

ROBIN RED BREAST
COME BACK COME BACK

After I touch the egg
my sister yells
as she runs off,

"She'll never come back.
The smell of your skin's
too scary." And so

I stay, waiting
for mother robin,
singing, *Come back*.

Come back.
The egg's not cracked.
I only fingered it,

rolling the smooth
speckled blue,
a little.

MIGRATION

This evening the geese keep coming.
My sister and I escape supper
to watch flock after flock leave. The leaders
fly them forward. The uplift
of wings pushes them on as one V
after another leaves us behind
with the cold already settled
into the ground waiting for the first snow.

My sister shouts how we too will go as the rush
of flight rises in our arms, stretched out
as we run, envying the flocks' instinct —
how they know when to leave, when to return —
until we tilt homeward, arms drooping with doubt.
Who will we follow? And will we ever go?

THE TEST

It's not yet dawn. My sister and I study
before our final exams — French for me,

History for her — how King Henry the Eighth
murdered his wives, the Wars of the Roses —

only a little of our own history here. At least
we speak the language I am declining.

We see the sun rise as we sink deeper
into our books, the blanket we share on the sofa.

In the next room our parents sleep, the youngest
still in the crib next to them. We study on,

turning pages as the light begins to grow
becoming the moment to close our books

and go on alone — the test of what we know.

MANITOBA

THE ICE AGE

Sometimes I think of the ice age, the glacier
covering our farm, scratching striations into rock,
sifting debris and dumping silt, the pressure
of movement and crazy currents cutting
and filling channels. It was the last retreat
of the continental ice sheet, shaping the land
to lines of natural force, making a geography
of place where I had no place yet, but a future

when a family might stake out a farm,
when a daughter might walk through a field
sifting handfuls of soil for fossils, or picking rocks
from freshly turned earth, to touch the thrust
of movement scratched in granite, to hold
the ice age, past and trembling, in my hand.

LAND

When he died   some of the children
and some   of the grandchildren
polished   the pemmican pounders
and flint arrowheads   my grandfather
collected from his field   to store in a toolshed
with greasy wrenches   and rusted bolts
while others lay   them in the ground
next to his body   Manitoba
Great Spirit's   Strait marked
by railroad surveyors   and government
workers giving   away land
our farm   staked out

IN THE MIDDLE OF
ANOTHER WINTER

the days always end like this. In crusty snow
and choking cold we pick through her tracks,
infinity above and our mother ahead,
a tired shadow, calling home the cows, looking back
to see her girls, laughter strangled by cold,
sink in her tracks. I see now
how we watched everything and how she selected
in lonely light the gestures to teach,
the ones to hold back: the steady pull on the teat,
the udders slackening one by one,
the swaying cows delivering milk, a half-ton of animal
backed into her, the trap of an animal ritual
with three daughters to raise. When I think of this,
the snow gives way and the light drifts on
in blues and greys. I think I'm alone
and I want to touch myself: the deep sea of stars,
the chattering girls and aching cows,
call home myself, the tired shadow.

THE OFFERING

Across the fence line
the tractor circles away from him.

It could have been
the first tragedy of our family —

our 2-year-old brother, never found,
wandered away one summer day.

Instead, our father found him
curled in a furrow, limp from the sun,

and carried him home,
running all the way

like a god
with an offering snatched from the field.

WHEAT

The sun soaks the field
forcing seeds to sprout
in neat coils of green.
By July the shoots
are up to our waist, stalks
rustling against dry winds.
Another month and fat pods
burst to the ground
as we rush to harvest,
the glory of wheat
pouring from our hands.

THE FIELD IN WINTER

When I think of the field
in winter, I feel lost.
I feel the first full moon
of the new year sharpen its light
against the cold. Razor-edged
metallic blue, it's everywhere.
Even in the warm room
where I dream of escape,
flailing in snow up to my hips.

THE FLAX FIELD
IN FLOWER

was our mirage of blue
sweeping low-lying lands
a false lake blooming
overnight receding
to dull stalks
stripped for cloth, and seeds
squeezed for oil, the mirage returning
in the cloth covering a feast
and the oil clearing a painter's mix.

RIGHT HERE

I want to tell you how the field at midnight
stretches into silence as the snow

glows blue against the full moon and how,
close to the ground, the colour doesn't matter

when you look up and lose everything
to thick stars, some falling, and northern lights

shifting as icebergs drift far far away.
Come to the point, you'll say

and I'll know this is the point, right here.

WEATHER

The wheat
rattles a warning
as it bends
flat to the ground.
Across the field,
a tree snaps. Today
the truth is in the wind
and in the sky
turning over black clouds.

THE LONGING OF IT

I am thinking of a single tree,
an oak tree from my childhood farm,
a tree the neighbour cut up one day
to make way for more cropland —
not greed exactly,
only a shallow kind of necessity.
All these years and I still have the image
of a single tree
rolling through my time
like a radio wave rolling
through deep space. Why? The image,
not the tree, survives as a phantom limb
I feel stirring from time to time
never knowing why, knowing
only the longing of it.

VANISHING POINT

It's a trick
of painting, lines
pierce the canvas, carry
the image beyond the frame,
even beyond museum walls where the image,
reversed and released, drifts across avenues, grazes
the head of the crowd and leaves the city grid,
expands over thickening trees,
thunders to meet galaxies
all while the eye
is open.

AERIAL VIEW

It turned up at a country fair. My brother,
flipping through photos, recognized the house
then the school bus in the yard. He looked hard
at the aerial view and made out our father
walking to the barn with children scattered
at the edge of the field. Now handsomely framed
the photo hangs in my living room where I stand
reeling through the flattened view to a place

I once thought silent and made for me
in shades of grey though now I see
colours and hear noises everywhere — brown earth
turned to a pristine sky, our father's shirt
a red blot against the barn faded red, and cicadas
droning with a plane thrumming overhead.

DEAR LAND

Grieving from bedrock
And unploughed fields
Grieve me sister
Mother grieve
Ashes and earth
Great stone
Rolled back empty

AFTER YEARS

IN EFFIGY

Do you know that ten years ago, from this jetty
I drowned you in effigy — a plain wooden box

carrying a strange cargo — a clay figure
oddly shaped, bits of cloth and a few words

shoved off to sea? That day
was not a good day. Cold, windy, the flat rocks

slick with rain, I almost slipped
into the grey water half hoping (or dreading?)

an answer to a call. And now, the light is clear,
the air warm for September as I walk

by carcasses of horseshoe crabs and gulls
sifting through seaweeds recalling another ocean

with your story of whales, calving in Baja. "All night,"
you said, "the whales kept calling, calling

to each other." On a clear day like today
I know the sounds I'll never hear

as I walk to the end of the jetty, stepping
from flat rock to flat rock

noticing twin gouges in the granite
where the rock was blasted from the earth.

AFTER YEARS

the minutes in between
become a long pool
of shallow water
reflecting
empty chairs
in black granite

THINK SLOWLY

and with great care
of the mind
crawling through dust
wanting a piece
of solid ground
just one step
in a crumbling staircase

ANOTHER PLACE

How you come back
in dreams
where I pull away

from light
to wrench
words from the dark

looking to find
and bring to an end
as every morning

the dreams
end on their own
with light

filtering
through the shutters
of our house

REMNANTS

It's what I have left to offer you —
   the ripple of a flax field in flower
the flow of a river slipping to sea
   the weight of a whale flipping over.
Say it's images from a life left over
   or the lust of memory
wanting its place of origin
   before the blue fades, before
the heft and swiftness disappear.

BLESSED

The whales surround us as a child
yelps in her father's arms, a pup
caught in the spray from the blowhole.
I can't help it. I feel blessed

by her cries, the whales'
rolling turns, the flip of a fluke
and the slippery disappearance
of mammoths into the deep.

WHAT'S PRESERVED

I'm standing on the silvered deck
of a house on the North Shore
looking over a bird preserve

with poles jutting over treetops,
nesting platforms
built for ospreys. The birds

want dead standing trees to nest
but everywhere here there's new growth
so the rangers build the platforms

as a way to keep the birds
from vanishing. And they come —
just now a pair circling in, wide

drooping wings, each with a fish
clutched headfirst, disappearing
into their nest where the feed begins.

The more I look the more I think
of what vanishes and what's preserved,
how I measure what's lost, a feather

lightly coloured, a sharp call, wings
resting in close, or closer yet, your face
resting in thought, your hands

sifting through the pages of a book
fading in the last light of day
as the ospreys rise for another dive.

THE LIFE OF THE MIND

The jellyfish lifts and sighs against the glass
while the shark swims a restless circle.

In the cheery tank next door
the dolphin chirps to the surface.

Outside, the beluga whale
swims straight to the crowd and fixes a girl

with her blue eye turned sideways.
That look could be

the life of the mind crossing over.
As the beluga looks on plainly, trailing the girl

behind the glass, the guide
explains a few whale facts — belugas

have good vision. Among all whales
they alone can turn their heads. Canaries of the sea,

belugas click, chirp and whistle to each other. This beluga
taught herself to make deep breathing sounds

and a bird call to the loon who lives above her
as if to say *listen, look, cross over, cross over*.

THE EDGE OF THE WORLD

The flat calm of the Pacific stunned us.
That afternoon, as my sister and I perched at the ocean's rim

it only seemed like the edge of the world.
We had just rolled a dying seal back to the surf

following a softly barked command
to touch once more the salt water.

I wiped my hands on my sister's shirt, the streak
marked her back like an ancient sign

of deliverance or grief
that time alone would make clear.

The seal raised a flipper
then floated belly up as we watched her disappear.

IT WAS NEVER MEANT

to be seen again. Built and buried
thirty years ago, the retaining wall never buckled
against its load. To the west, the river
pressing in and every day, straight above, the weight
of the building with ordinary thousands
riding elevators, walking office halls or studying faces
mirrored in windows. Now with the building
torn from its side, I see the wall, in bright daylight, crack open

from the river pressing in, the crack running up the street
until dazed engineers scrambling through rubble recall
posts and slabs below ground sturdy enough to tie back
the wall rising from the movement of a natural law,
the sudden release of half a load
and the force of gravity somehow making balance work.

RELEASE

We don't have to teach the girls how, the instinct
for snow play is already strong in their bones.

The youngest flips into a fresh bank — call it
"Red Suit in Pursuit of Snow Angel"—

as the oldest studies snow falling on her palm.
It's an ordinary evening in Brooklyn.

Fresh with snow, the whole street
is already scraping and shovelling, shifting piles

from here to there. Fathers
race down the street pulling sleds. Someone wins!

Someone loses.
Halfway down the street, someone

loses his bundle, the sled
suddenly gone light, the perfect moment

to pray for release, with the girls in the yard
building their tunnel, laughing from end to end.

Notes

Page 37
In section I, the passage in italics is from Georges Bataille quoted in Shoshana Felman *Writing and Madness (Literature / Philosophy / Psychoanalysis).* Cornell University Press: Ithaca, NY. 1985.

Page 42
The phrase "an illness like any other" is quoted from Vincent Van Gogh's letter to his brother Theo dated 1889. "As for me, you must know I shouldn't precisely have chosen madness if there had been any choice. What consoles me is that I am beginning to consider madness as an illness like any other, and that I accept it as such."
The passage in italics is quoted from Vincent Van Gogh's letter to his brother Theo dated March 30, 1888.

Page 45
"The Simplicity of Play" is a variation on a poem by Marie Howe, "Wanting a Child."

.

ACKNOWLEDGEMENTS

My thanks to the editors of the following publications, where some of these poems first appeared: *Barrow Street*, *The Cortland Review*, *The Malahat Review* and *September 11, 2001: American Writers Respond*.

Heartfelt thanks to Beth Follett for her vision as a publisher; to Molly Peacock for her generous reading of these poems; and to Zab for her ever artful design.

Loving thanks to my daughters, and to my husband David Koosis, my first and most trusted reader.

PHOTO Galilea Nin

Rachel Vigier is the author of *Gestures of Genius: Women, Dance, and the Body* (The Mercury Press, 1994). She was raised on a farm in Manitoba and now lives with her family in New York City. *On Every Stone* is her first collection of poems.